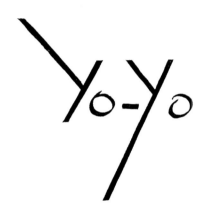

Kidnapped
in
Provence

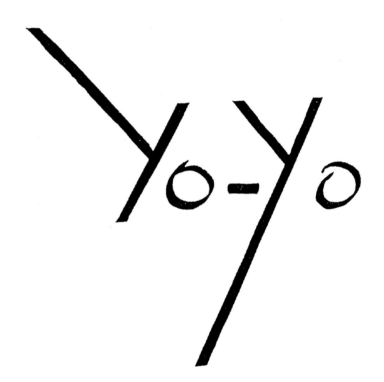

Kidnapped
in
Provence

DAVID DOUGLAS DUNCAN

Château La Coste - Vintage Edition

Photography / Text /
Design / Production: David Douglas Duncan
Manuscript computer composition: Franck Follet, Antibes
Final computer manuscript : Jef Regnier, Opio
Secret-camera photos: Franck Follet, Antibes
Secret-camera ultra prints: LIFE photo-lab, New York
Imagined Yo-Yo kidnapping / ransoming: Baroness Ariane van der Elst

Printed and bound in Italy by Mondadori of Verona

Contents

Three months old   His first photo — he bit me

Thor, the most noble of German Shepherds,
graced our home for fourteen years —
smitten one night by his loss.

But then,
rogue spirits in a born rebel
restored that wasteland —
with laughter we hoped forever.

We had named him Yankee Yoshii
for our homeland and a friend.

Immediately,
defying both gravity and reality
he catapulted into orbit
where he renamed himself.

One month at home

Their Secret Island was Themselves

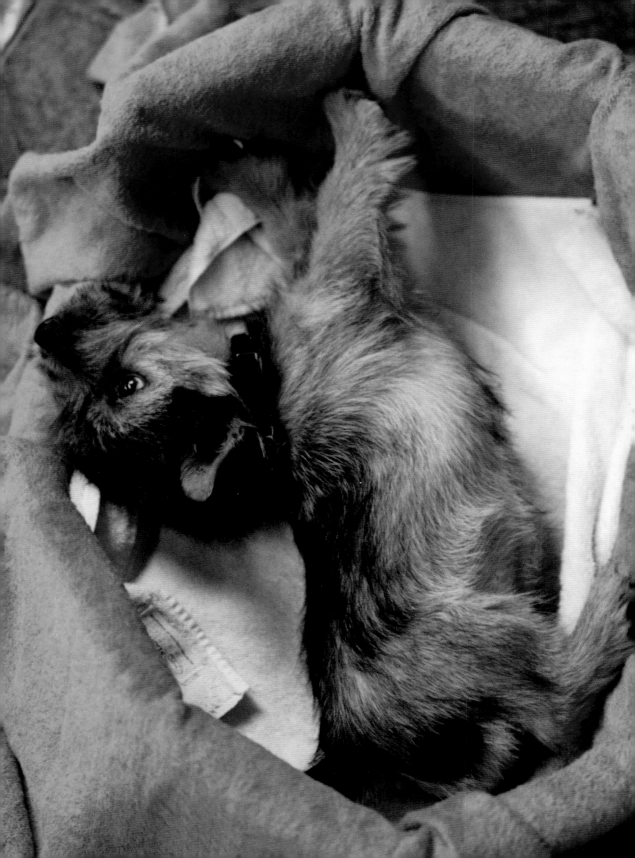

Tattooed Innocence

Kidnapped!

Gone . . . Yo-Yo with car . . . midnight,
serene village in southern France.

Long-awaited dinner with Kansas City childhood friends a catastrophe.

Raining — tiny police post empty. Choking on anger; stupidity of leaving Yo
asleep alone on cushions instead of in the restaurant. Sick with apprehension,
seeing him being thrown from our stolen car into a merciless night.

Our Prayer

Yo-Yo's immediate empathy with strangers would seduce one of
his abductors who would take him home, where we somehow might find him.

First photo with Yo-Yo

One Man's War

Fighting Shadows
in
Legendary Landscapes

Speed . . . instant response was *everything!*

Picasso was my talisman for finding Yo-Yo. After reporting Yo's theft to nearby St. Rémy police (renting a car for the two-hour drive home) my battle strategy became clear. I phoned old-friend Serge Assier, photo-boss at *Le Provencal*, Marseille's powerhouse newspaper that blankets every niche of Provence.

Asking (never before) to be interviewed. Immediately! Guided by a veteran war photographer's radar. Our new Audi, matt-silver stationwagon, had been stolen by rogue local Gypsies. Picasso was almost godlike for all Gypsies. I was a friend of Picasso. I would post a massive no questions "reward" ransom for Yo-Yo. Serge put me on hold. Within a couple of minutes: "David, you're set for our art editor — ten tomorrow. Bring a closeup shot with Yo-Yo."

Black-belt Judo   Camera Fanatic   Digital Printer

Le Provençal

On a volé le chien de David Douglas Duncan

Le grand photographe David Douglas Duncan est au désespoir. "Yankee Yoshii", le norwich terrier de 4 mois qu'il avait laissé, un court instant, dans sa voiture garée lundi soir à Maussane (Bouches-du-Rhône) a disparu, aux mains du ou des voleurs du véhicule. Seule, ladite voiture a été retrouvée (volant cassé, direction forcée) le lendemain à l'Ile-sur-Sorgue.

David Douglas Duncan lance un appel pressant et offre une très forte récompense à toute personne qui lui permettra de retrouver "Yankee Yochii", un cadeau d'anniversaire à son épouse Sheila, pour remplacer "Thor", le berger allemand auquel le photographe de Picasso et des stars mondiales a consacré un magnifique album. Détail important : le petit chien porte un tatouage.

Pour tout renseignement, s'adresser au "Provençal" à Serge Assier. ☎ 91 84 47 91. D'avance, merci.

One Gifted Man

Twenty-four hours later *Provencal's* appeal became a reward-ransom poster. Carbon-steel tough and just out of the French Army, Franck Follet designed and had printed hundreds of four-color posters. That same day gendarmes found our damaged Audi — not Yo — filled with anti-auto theft promotional handbooks whose local agent's address was listed as near Marseille. He told Sheila (our French-language expert) that his company's demo-car loaded with their anti-theft devices had also been stolen while he was having coffee with some clients. He heard *his* alarms explode, rushed out — stopped. His stationwagon had been tail-bashed by a silver Audi, breaking its anti-theft locks. He was also facing a circle of unsmiling eyes and barely hidden weapons. He watched as his bumper-sagging, anti-theft, hi-tech university-on-wheels disappeared with its gangster escort . . . and I knew my foe.

Yo-Yo was instant news   His ransom was ready from Day One

10,000 FRANCS REWARD
TO WHOEVER FINDS "YANKEE YOSHII"
MY LITTLE FRIEND

Le PROVENCAL

Someone has stolen the dog of
David Douglas Duncan

Veteran photographer David Douglas Duncan is in despair. Yankee Yoshii, the 4-month-old Norwich terrier that he had briefly left in his car in the village of Maussane (Bouches-du-Rhone) was taken by a robber or robbers who stole his vehicle last Monday. Only the car was found with a broken steering wheel the next day at l'Ile-sur-Sorgue.

David Douglas Duncan is offering a substantial reward and appealing to anyone who may be able to help him find Yankee Yoshii. The puppy was a birthday gift to his wife Sheila to replace Thor, a German Shepherd, by the photographer of world-famous stars and Picasso. The little dog can be identified by his tattoo.

For information contact Serge Assier
Le Provencal - Phone: 91 84 47 91

Marseille $2000 Reward

Fellow Photographers as Weapons

Le Provencal's story became the message in our search for Yo-Yo. Against all advice — gendarmes, journalists, his vet: "*Never* reveal your actual reward with a poster!" I gambled, hoping to make immediate contact with his abductors. Money in excess of anyone's wildest dream the night he and our car were stolen.

Three contact phones were listed on Yo's poster.

Two, were of the Marseille and Nice newspapers that ran his story. The third, was the home of our neighbors Audrey and Bobby Billam, who had shared Yo-Yo's loss from the start, then joined our poster campaign to find him.

And the corrosive waiting began —

Serge Assier   "Shoot your story . . . Watch for Yo-Yo"

Darkroom souvenirs of exhibits

Counterattack!

Vincent also battled shadows in Arles at the "Night Cafe." Just the place to launch our poster war for Yo-Yo. Immediate good luck! Lucien Clergue was at home in Arles. Born there. Honored by the *Guide Michelin* like a national monument. Founder of Arles' annual International Photography Conference. Also, photographer of Picasso — godfather of his daughter. Revered by Gypsies. They and Picasso, I hoped, would lead us to Yo-Yo.

"Leave Yo-Yo's posters!"   "They will be seen!"

"The grandchildren will put them everywhere"

Gypsy Matriarch

Clementine Reyes: the mother of lengendary Manitas de Plata, leader of the Camargue Gypsy Kings guitarists, Clergue's lifelong cronies.

As a child, Lucien had played in the debris of millennia strewn everywhere around Arles. His friends of the heart — from origins just as ancient — were children of the Gypsy clans in the Camargue, a marsh-wilderness wonderland just south of town. Picasso invited me to hear them when Lucien brought Manitas de Plata and The Gypsy Kings to his studio, where they fired barrage after barrage such as I had never heard before — not "music"— *cannonades* of respect from another world. Picasso called for and signed each guitar.

Arles
Two thousand-year-old Roman arena

Maussane-les-Apilles
Village church

Kidnapped in Provence

Cézanne painted Ste. Victoire: the mountain became the art world's Mount Everest. Peter Mayle wrote "A Year in Provence" and a remote Luberon valley became a tour-bus parking lot. Van Gogh came to Arles, painted the postman, a chair, his favored cafe and brutalizing self-portraits; all in volcanic colors that left him penniless, but later ignited the imagination of mankind — and made Arles the romantic pulse of Provence. It was here, that our village neighbors Audrey Billam and her towering son, Bobby, joined Yo-Yo's poster blitz in a bone-numbing mistral, with Baba their elderly lady Norwich terrier under one arm; then day-after-day while everybody searched for Yo.

Farm-family vegetables

Maussane-les-Alpilles

Church-square market day

Veteran shepherd

Village venders

All agreed: "Stolen here — Search here."

Village policeman

"No . . . nobody with that face — so small!"

"But he's welcome."

"Yes! Yes! We will all watch for Yo-Yo."

Yoshii Gallery
Paris

Yoshii Château
Cévennes

Museum-Art-World Tycoon

Chozo Yoshii / Yo's godfather
on phone

"Please place the Yo-Yo poster at the gallery front door for your exhibit."

Opening night / equal billing

Yo's friend abstract expressionist artist Paul

30,000,000 + One
Trente Million d'Amis

Host Jean-Pierre Hutin had never aired such a story. "Imagine the pets lost and stolen everyday!" Reha, his producer-wife, made my "friend of Picasso" pitch. Finally, her ace-of-aces: She had often vacationed in our village. (Turkish teenager who turned all heads.) Yo was her friend! Her message covered France, much of Europe and England, every Saturday night.

Reha Kutlu-Hutin, Yo-Yo's poolside pal   Heidi Goulandris, Yo-Yo's neighbor

PARIS MATCH
63 Champs-Elysees

Michel looked at me, then at my shots
of Yo-Yo. "David, you're an old LIFE
photographer. This is MATCH!"

"Who runs stolen-dog pictures?"

"Until now!"

"Korea! . . . Vietnam . . . *a war story!*"

He smiled.

"Picasso helps."

Michel Sola: editor-in-chief

"Find Yo-Yo!" — "Touch their hearts!"

Response was awesome. Sola, everyone at MATCH had to toss aside everything basic in big-time journalism to publish Yo-Yo's story as a hometown tear jerker. Picasso indeed was vital. But the secret of that appeal for help lay hidden deep in the hearts of those men who late one autumn afternoon rewrote the law, to help a foreigner find his stolen dog.

PARIS MATCH

DAVID DOUGLAS DUNCAN A PERDU YANKEE YOSHII

Sa renommée mondiale ne peut le consoler : David Douglas Duncan, l'un de plus grands

Contact!

"I've got your dog."

"He's asleep with my little girl."

"She calls him Jimmy."

Unflappable, affable, and always articulate in English and French. Australian-born Bobby Billam took the call. Their home phone was on Yo-Yo's poster. Muffled voice confirmed Yo's tattoo. Demanded quintupled ransom. Knew his cards but settled for less.

I told Bobby: "Pay . . . Get Yo-Yo!"

The voice: "No *flics!*" (cops). "But of course — no flics!" / "Saturday 1400 supermarket north of Marseille front-door parking . . . no flics!"

Marseille suburb

13 minutes

We arrived in the parking area exactly at 1400, barely moving. Sheila, Audrey, Bobby and Baba — while I wondered how many eyes were tracking us as we parked. Opposite the supermarket front door — knowing armed veterans were searching for *anything* that revealed our duplicity. Saw a dozen shadows — well positioned (professional). Got out . . . Sheila, Audrey, Bobby and Baba stayed in the car — while I waited.

Met *him*: Slender, bronzed, unshaven, thirtyish; cap brim low over unblinking coffee-dregs eyes. Unbuttoned, slightly bulged jacket. (Like mine; an old friend from World War II, Korea and Vietnam over my heart.) Shook hands. I asked about Yo in what he mistook for French. He left-hand pointed to a distant battered white BMW. "Bring him here!" (my left hand). And he did while I posted myself between a couple of cars — with his nearest cover behind me at the super-market front door. With Yo in sight, time to check the perimeter — about twenty-odd goons. Yo-Yo's ransom seemed fair. I had put it in books. "The Private World of Picasso" for him. The second book, about Thor, was for his daughter who probably loved and now surely missed "Jimmy." He waved aside count-ing that ransom; just aimed those cap-shielded eyes at me, and maybe smiled. Then walked back to the crowded BMW, my books in his right hand. I passed Yo-Yo to Sheila — bought bouquets for her and Audrey from a flower-lady in front of the market; enough time for everyone to relax, light up, and follow the BMW.

Supermarket "shoppers" everywhere ready to ambush one happy ex-Marine

Korea . . . Vietnam?

Confrontation — Pay off — Liberation

"YANKEE YOSHII" MON PETIT AMI

P.S.C. 300
TATOUAGE

Le Provencal

On a volé le chien de David Douglas Dun...

Le grand photographe David Douglas Duncan est... poir. "Yankee Yoshii", le norwich terrier de 4 mois qu'il... sé, un court instant, dans sa voiture garée lundi soir à... (Bouches-du-Rhône) a disparu, aux mains du ou des... véhicule. Seule, ladite voiture a été retrouvée (volant c... tion forcée) le lendemain à l'Ile-sur-Sorgue.

David Douglas Duncan lance un appel pressant... très forte récompense à toute personne qui lui perm... trouver "Yankee Yochii", un cadeau d'anniversaire à... Sheila, pour remplacer "Thor", le berger allemand a... tographe de Picasso et des stars mondiales a consac... fique album. Détail important : le petit chien porte...

Pour tout renseignement, s'adresser au "Prove... Assier. ☎ 91 84 47 91. D'avance, merci.

RENSEIGNEMENTS AU 93 75 24 23
LE PROVENCAL : 91 84 47 91 - NICE MATIN : 93 85...

(left column, partially visible)
chien
...as Duncan

...glas Duncan est au déses-
...r de 4 mois qu'il avait lais-
...arée lundi soir à Maussane
...ains du ou des voleurs du
...trouvée (volant cassé, direc-
...Sorgue.

...appel pressant et offre une
...ne qui lui permettra de re-
...d'anniversaire a son epouse
...ger allemand auquel le pho-
...ndiales a consacré un magni...
...petit chien porte un tatouage.

...sser au "Provençal" à Serge
...erci.

...23
...N : 93 85 67 68

10.000 F
A QUI RETROUVERA...

(left) F ...ERA

"YANKEE YOSHII" MON P...

(bottom left) ...N PETIT AMI

P.S.C. 300

"You found him"

She was ravaged by that nineteen-day vigil. Was he sick, hungry, hurt, abandoned; locked in a cellar tortured by weirdos; used for experiments; dead? Her constant prayer was that he be safe, fed, loved. All of this, and more, was in her exhausted face. She held him close, alone.

L'Ile-sur-Sorgue

National Gendarmerie
Reporting Yo-Yo's recovery

"Nobody laughs
or gets kissed very often
around this place."

Captain Franck Dupas.

"It's like a school reunion — maybe a wedding — never happened before in these headquarters."

Yo-Yo's lucky star was Picasso

When Yo-Yo saw another Norwich in my arms he bristled, groaning with fury . . . maybe at me. André Villers, my fellow-photographer friend in nearby hilltop Mougins had recorded the entire *Trente Million d'Amis* program to surprise Sheila and me. Picasso watched from over her shoulder — one of André's prints of *his* neighbor on another hilltop just across the road. The photograph was appropriate: Picasso had been Yo-Yo's lucky star from that first night when he was stolen.

Yo-Yo got a freedom kiss from Franck Follet when I took this documentary shot of the little ex-hostage with his poster — then Franck dropped a 35mm-film casette in my hand. He had followed us into that gangster trap, parked, and shot the entire ransoming of Yo through his windshield with a wide-angle Nikon hidden under a newspaper. He apologized that he missed the shot when I turned from the gang leader with Yo-Yo in my arms: "David, his guys were right beside me. They would have heard my shutter if I fired . . . I'm sorry!"

Friends at LIFE's photo-lab in New York took his film and used a NASA space-enlarger to extract precise images from 12-foot projections on the darkroom floor — Marseille, again, for me.

Our Belgian Baroness neighbor Ariane's lady Corsican donkey welcomed Yo in her garden where she had posed her own Cairn terrier when drawing the kidnapping of Yo-Yo and his life as Gypsy "Jimmy".

Younger neighbors, Sonia and Luke Mc Clure, hugged miserable Yo-Yo, and their Humphrey, in a joyous "Welcome home!" waltz — unaware of his pain. A sadist abductor had tried to conceal his stomach tattoo under acid-burn scars.

Village Pals

"Welcome home Monsieur Yo-Yo"
Mohammed - Ahmed - André

Nineteen Days

The
Last Leaves
of
Yo-Yo's
First Autumn

His Birthday
Five Months Old

Celebration!

Yo-Yo's 12th-birthday party (months)

Yo's neighbors: Ike, Rambo . . . and
misguided Kirby

Pretending to disappear
but
never
out of sight

Inseparable shadow

His World was in His Eyes

Every day — Every night

As with Thor
Fourteen Years of Love

Then — Again
"Goodbye"